Diminishing Resources
Forests

Diminishing Resources
Forests

Allen Stenstrup

MORGAN REYNOLDS PUBLISHING

Greensboro, North Carolina

Diminishing Resources
SERIES

Soil | Forests | Water | Oil

Diminishing Resources: Forests

Library of Congress Cataloging-in-Publication Data

Stenstrup, Allen.
  Diminishing resources. Forests / by Al Stenstrup.
     p. cm.
  Includes bibliographical references and index.
  ISBN 978-1-59935-116-2 (alk. paper)
  1. Forests and forestry--Juvenile literature. 2. Deforestation--Juvenile
literature. 3. Sustainable forestry--Juvenile literature. I. Title.
  SD376.S74 2009
  333.75--dc22
                                        2009031025

Printed in the United States of America
First Edition

*To the students and teachers of the Peten
Region of Guatemala who learn and work
daily to sustain their community forests*

Contents

Chapter One
The Forest Planet

Each year, one of the most phenomenal migrations on
earth takes place when hundreds of millions of monarch butterflies fly from east of the Rocky Mountains
and southern Canada to a winter refuge in the oyamel fir forests of central Mexico.

A monarch butterfly weighs, on average, about half a
gram—less than a paper clip—yet, these fragile insects fly
up to 3,000 miles from their summer breeding grounds, in
milkweed fields, to remote mountaintops in Mexico, where
the states of Mexico and Michoacan meet. They will remain
there from mid-November until mid-February, when temperatures rise.

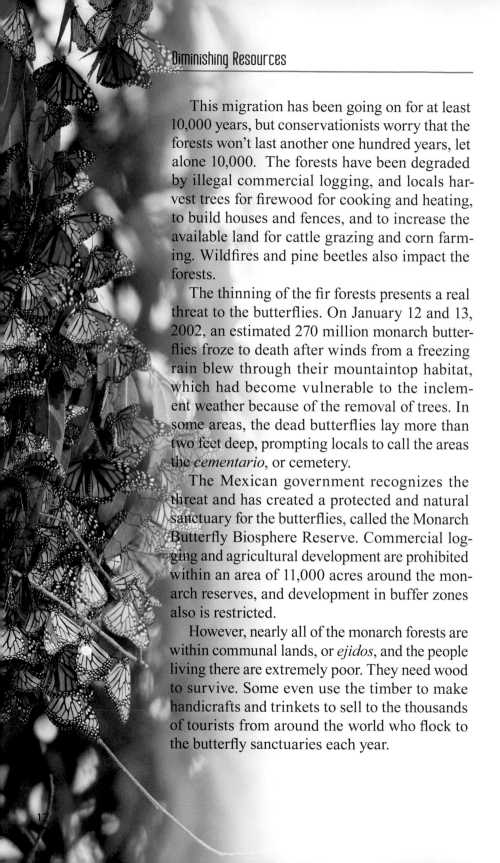

This migration has been going on for at least 10,000 years, but conservationists worry that the forests won't last another one hundred years, let alone 10,000. The forests have been degraded by illegal commercial logging, and locals harvest trees for firewood for cooking and heating, to build houses and fences, and to increase the available land for cattle grazing and corn farming. Wildfires and pine beetles also impact the forests.

The thinning of the fir forests presents a real threat to the butterflies. On January 12 and 13, 2002, an estimated 270 million monarch butterflies froze to death after winds from a freezing rain blew through their mountaintop habitat, which had become vulnerable to the inclement weather because of the removal of trees. In some areas, the dead butterflies lay more than two feet deep, prompting locals to call the areas the *cementario*, or cemetery.

The Mexican government recognizes the threat and has created a protected and natural sanctuary for the butterflies, called the Monarch Butterfly Biosphere Reserve. Commercial logging and agricultural development are prohibited within an area of 11,000 acres around the monarch reserves, and development in buffer zones also is restricted.

However, nearly all of the monarch forests are within communal lands, or *ejidos*, and the people living there are extremely poor. They need wood to survive. Some even use the timber to make handicrafts and trinkets to sell to the thousands of tourists from around the world who flock to the butterfly sanctuaries each year.

There is hope, though, for the mountaintop forests. The Mexican government and numbers of nongovernmental organizations are working to preserve and restore the once-pristine forests, by encouraging locals to engage in ecotourism, trout farming, and other industries, instead of logging and growing corn or oats. And in some areas, thousands of trees have been planted. In 2008, one group managed to plant 740,000 trees, which will go a long way in restoring the climate and habitat for the butterflies.

Forests are vital to life on Earth. They cleanse the air, protect the water in rivers and streams, stabilize soil, control flooding, and prevent drought. Forests are the home of the largest reservoir of biological diversity, containing more than 70 percent of all the world's flora and fauna. They purify the air we breathe and prevent erosion of soil. Valuable resources that sustain our society, lifestyle, and health like wood, paper, and medicinal plants all come from forests. They are also the home of 60 million people who depend on forests for their daily survival, and worldwide an estimated 1.6 billion people depend on the forest for their livelihoods. Yet, each year the world loses nearly 36 million acres of natural forest—about twenty football fields lost every minute. Almost all of this loss is caused by human activities.

The Food and Agriculture Organization of the United Nations (FAO), the leading source of information on the status of the world's forests, defines forest as land with a tree canopy cover of more than 10 percent and an area of more than one

acre. It is important to understand that there are many different kinds of forests. A primary forest has never been logged, has developed under natural processes, and has its native tree species. Seminatural forests are managed forests modified by man through forest management (silviculture) and assisted regeneration. A secondary forest is a forest that has regrown after a major disturbance such as fire, timber harvest, disease damage, or wind damage, so that the effects of the disturbance are no longer visible.

For thousands of years, humans have impacted forests. We have always cut down trees for firewood and the making of shelters. We have used wood for making weapons and tools. Much of that impact was minor, when populations were low and the impact on the overall forests was minimal. Today, it is a different story and with a different result.

The total forest area of planet Earth is about 15.2 million square miles. This is roughly 30 percent of the earth's land area. It is estimated that about one half of the forests that covered the Earth are now gone.

Staggering statistics from different parts of the world today give an indication of what is happening to the forests of the world.

More than 90 percent of West Africa's coastal rain forests have disappeared since 1900. According to the United Nations, "Africa is losing more than 9.9 million acres of forest every year—twice the world's average deforestation rate."

Not including the forests of Russia, only 1 percent of primary forests remain in Europe.

In 1970, the tropical rain forest of Brazil was largely untouched. Since that time, however, about 20 percent of the forest has been lost.

Haiti, an island country in the Caribbean and home to 8 million people, was once covered with forests. Today, only 2 percent remains forested. And conservationists fear that what has happened in Haiti is being repeated in the African country of Malawi. Cutting of trees to produce charcoal and to cure tobacco is leading to a sequence of events in Malawi that parallels that in Haiti. The forest area of this country of 13 million people has been reduced from 47 percent to 27 percent in just years.

The Chinese government has banned tree cutting in the Yangtze River basin. This decision came in 1998 after the region experienced flooding that caused more than $30

billion in damages and resulted in the loss of life of more than 3,000 people.

In 2004, Philippine President Gloria Macapagal-Arroyo ordered the military and police to crack down on illegal logging, after flash floods and landslides, triggered by deforestation, killed nearly 340 people.

At the beginning of the twentieth century, the earth's estimated forest area was about 19 million square miles. Today it is estimated at 15.2 million square miles—a loss of 20 percent. Of the forests that remain, the World Resources Institute estimates that only 22 percent of the world's primary forest cover remains intact, with most of this in three regions: the boreal forest of Canada and Alaska, the boreal forests of Russia, and the tropical rain forest of Brazil and other countries in South America.

Cold and snow dominate a boreal domain. The growing season is about 130 days and most of the precipitation falls in the form of snow. Temperatures vary from -58° F to 86° F. Eight or more months out of the year the mean monthly temperature is less then 50° F. The boreal forest is characterized by long winters, and snow may remain on the ground for as long as nine months in the northern regions of the boreal

forest. The earth's largest forests are the boreal forests, covering 4 million square miles of the earth's land surface.

The boreal forest accounts for more than one fourth of the earth's total forest area. They reach across the North American continent from Alaska to Newfoundland, Canada. In Europe they stretch from Scotland on the west to the tip of Siberia, Russia. Looking down at the North Pole, they form a circle around the earth, from the 50 degree to 70 degree latitudes of the planet. This is why they are sometimes referred to as "Earth's Green Crown." They measure a total of 6.5

Annual net change in forest area by region 1990-2005
(million ha per year)

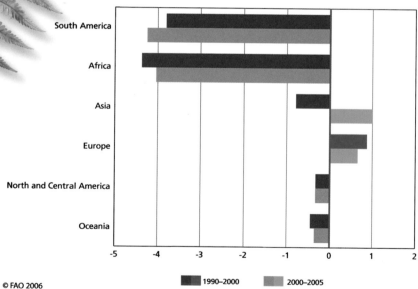

© FAO 2006

million square miles—about twice the size of the continental United States.

The sun barely rises in this region for many months. The summers, with no nighttime, provide for a short period of uninterrupted growth. The plants produce flowers and the insects live their life cycle very quickly. Still, the trees grow slowly, with Russian larches taking up to sixty years to grow an inch in diameter.

The term taiga is sometimes used to describe the northern, more barren, regions of the boreal forest. The most common tree species are the conifers like pine, spruce, larch, and fir. In the southern areas of the boreal forest you will also find deciduous trees like the aspen and birch.

The climate is cold and severe, so the population of people is very sparse in the region. Although the population is sparse, the impact of humans on this region is increasing. The boreal forest is a key factor in global carbon storage. The boreal region covers just 15 percent of the global land surface, but contains more than 30 percent of all the carbon in the terrestrial biome. This is mostly due to the cold temperatures that reduce the rate of decomposition, resulting in soils that are very old and rich in carbon. This makes the boreal forest a key factor in carbon storage for the planet, making it a vital regulator of the earth's climate.

The boreal forest is changing, though. The Canadian government owns 94 percent of the boreal forest found in Canada. Much of this land has been allotted to forest product companies that produce and supply paper for U.S. consumers. According to the Nature Conservancy, "Today, because of pressure for resources such as timber, hydroelectric power and minerals, Canada's boreal forest is being lost at a rate of about 1 percent a year. This rate of loss is similar to the pace of destruction in tropical rain forests."

Tropical forests have a mean temperature of more than 64°F each month. In other words, no winter. They are found mostly between the Tropic of Cancer (23° N Latitude) and the Tropic of Capricorn (23° S Latitude). Looking at the global map you can see a ring of forests around the equator. The three major regions of tropical forests can be found in South America, Africa, and Southeast Asia. Precipitation varies from the tropical deserts, where all months are dry, to the tropical rain forest, which has at least sixty inches of rain annually. In some areas of the rain forests, it may be as high as four hundred inches per year. It is no surprise then that the relative humidity in these forests stays between 75 and 100 percent.

Tropical rain forests are best known for their diversity of species, both flora and fauna. From the very large to the very small, many unique plants and animals are found in the rain forest. Common trees include ceiba, chicle, teak, mahogany, and cinchona. The high level of rainfall means the soil is in constant wetness. The rainfall leaches the soil of nutrients, and the plants take the nutrients up into the plant. Therefore most of the nutrients are in the plants. The fauna is also very unique. The flying frogs of Malaysia, for example, have extended toe tips and broadly webbed front and back feet and can glide from the tops of tall trees.

The tropical rain forests are facing major changes today. Illegal logging and slash-and-burn agriculture are two of the leading causes of deforesation in the tropical forests.

Another type of forest, temperate forests, are found on all continents, except Antarctica. They can be found between 30-50 degrees latitude in both hemispheres, but most are found in the Northern Hemisphere. These regions have a mean monthly temperature of more than 50°F between four and eight months of the year. Precipitation varies greatly within this domain.

Temperate forests have four seasons, ranging from cold average temperatures in winter to warm temperatures in summer. The trees and plants change with the seasons and many are adapted to forest fires that can occur in this region. Many of the trees "throw away" their leaves for the winter and produce a new crop of leaves when the buds burst open each spring. Conifers and deciduous trees make up the composition of the forest, with most being pines, oaks, beeches, and maple.

Human activities have had a tremendous impact on the temperate forest. The temperate forests of both Europe and North America have been greatly reduced with the expansion of agriculture. In Europe less than 2 percent of the primary forest still remains. In North America, most had been completely cleared by the beginning of the twentieth century. Secondary forests in these regions have replaced the primary forest.

The World's Forests

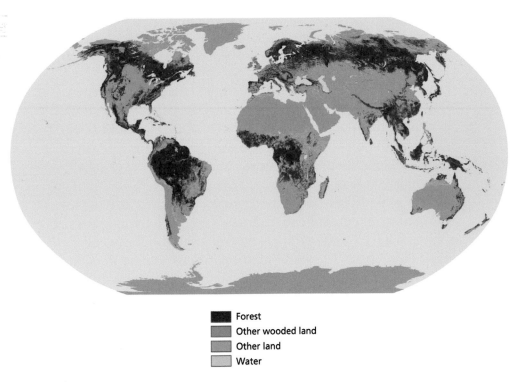

- Forest
- Other wooded land
- Other land
- Water

© FAO 2006

Afforestation: Planting It Big

Afforestation is defined as the planting of new forests on lands that historically have not contained forests. One country has preserved 115 million acres of afforestation, ranking it first in the world. That country is China. Since 1979, millions of Chinese citizens, civil servants, and state leaders take up shovels to plant trees on March 12, *nianjun*—the National Tree-Planting Day. For China and the world, it is the largest annual tree-planting event. The day stresses the importance of trees and also fulfills a legal duty for every citizen over the age of eleven to plant at least three trees every year. "China plants more trees than the rest of the world combined," says John McKinnon, the head of the EU-China Biodiversity Programme. By some estimates, the Chinese plant 5 billion trees a year.

Many are planted in the northern shelterbelt, also known as the Great Green Wall. Started in November 1978, the goal of the tree belt is to stretch 2,688 miles, from outer Beijing through Inner Mongolia. It is designed to protect cities and cropland from floods and the desert. It is the largest ecological project in the world, and the mass tree-planting will give China the biggest artificial forest in the world, covering an area twice the size of Britain.

The goal of the afforestation project is to slow or reverse the process of desertification. In the last one hundred years, China, with 1.3 billion mouths to feed each day, has needed agricultural land. The world's most populous country thought little of cutting down its forests. The forests were cleared to provide new farmland to feed the growing urban population. The tremendous expansion of the mass iron and steel smelting campaign further required wood for fuel. China also needed the timber to construct buildings and the cleared land to build on. This widespread deforestation led to major changes across China. Hillsides and steep slopes, now bare of trees, were

Volunteer tree planters in Hong Kong work with seedlings from an evergreen tree that reaches 120 feet tall, with a spread half as wide. Due to its fire resistant qualities, the *Schima superba* is often used for building firebreaks in south China to help control forest fires.

unable to trap rainfall. This contributed to increased runoff and summer floods that would often kill thousands of people along the rivers of China, in particular, the Yangtze River. ■

Chapter Two
Deforestation: The Human Impact

E ight thousand years ago, a booming farm-based civilization appeared in the area encompassing the Nile, Tigris,
and Euphrates river valleys. This civilization thrived for
more than 3,000 years, but then disappeared. Recent excava-
tions indicate that the reason for its downfall was deforestation.
"It seems that the people cut the oak forests of the area for
housing, and overgrazing by goat herds prevented the forest
from regrowing. Without tree cover, the soils deteriorated and

farming became impossible," explains David A. Perry, professor (emeritus) in the Department of Forest Science at Oregon State University.

In the South Pacific, Easter Island is famously studded with enormous stone head statues. The island was lushly forested when Polynesians first settled there 1,000 years ago. Then, according to geography professor Jared Diamond, author of *Collapse: How Societies Choose to Fail or Succeed*, "the settlers of Easter Island proceeded to chop down trees for the same reason that we and all other people chop down trees: They chopped them for fuel for cooking. Chopped them for firewood to warm themselves. Chopped them down for construction. . . . Chopped them down to make levers to transport and erect the giant statues. They chopped them down to make dugout canoes." As the forest disappeared, the land became exposed to wind and water erosion and could no longer sustain the growing population. The quality of life for the Islanders plummeted, chaos set in, and the population crashed.

Throughout history, a pattern of rising population, deforestation, soil loss, and scarcity has been repeated over and over again around the world. Scientists estimate that about half of the world's original forest has been lost, with some regions of the world losing a much higher percentage. Most of this loss has been due to humans. "The spread of agriculture and domesticated animals, increasing population and cutting of forests for timber and fuel have all taken their toll," author Peter Thomas wrote in *Ecology of Woodland and Forests*.

It is clear that deforestation is not new. However, in the last 150 years—and especially in the last fifty years—it has reached new levels. In many parts of the world, deforestation is occurring at an alarming rate, and forests have all but disappeared in twenty-five different countries.

Deforestation is the permanent clearing of a natural forest or woodland, and people have always cut trees for a variety of uses. As Perry explains, "People have been deforesting the Earth since we first became farmers and townspeople." The

causes of deforestation today are similar to the ones on Easter Island hundreds of years ago. People continue to cut trees for housing and fuel, they use the logs for a variety of tools and materials, and they clear forest to make way for farming and livestock grazing.

However, the sheer numbers of people doing these things today has grown exponentially, and the rising population means an ever-increasing impact on the world's forests. In addition, most people today use materials and consume goods at a rate that would have been unimaginable to Easter Islanders. Beyond the simple things needed for survival, people all over the world buy countless products made of raw materials either from forests or from areas that were once forests.

(continued on page 34)

Global Wood Products

Wood has been an important raw material from the earliest societies to our daily use of products today. Used in the manufacturing of products from the tiny toothpick to furniture to large buildings, it contributes $468 billion to the world's economy. It is the primary source or material for construction. Wood is the dominant resource used in single-family and low-rise multifamily construction. Wood is also critical for the shipping of all products, because they are shipped on wood palates.

Wood also provides the raw material needed by the pulp and paper industry. Trees are harvested and converted to wood chips. The chips are reduced to pulp in the paper-making process. Pulp is composed of cellulose, long chains of sugar molecules which make up the cell walls. The combination of raw pulp and recycled paper produces various types of paper that impact people's lives every day.

Wood provides us with additional by-products. These are valuable products that can be extracted from wood. Wood fuel for energy is grouped into this category. Forests also bring us products that are not wood. These non-wood products, such as medicine and berries, provide resources for many populations of people, both for subsistence living and economic endeavors. According to the UN's Food and Agriculture Organization, "the production and consumption of wood products and wood energy are expected to increase, largely following historical trends. The most rapid growth will occur from the emerging economies of China and India." ∎

Pictured here is a hillside housing construction site at Costa del Sol, Spain.

These two things—rising population and increased consumerism—are the underlying causes for almost all the deforestation occurring today. There are also many direct causes of deforestation, including replacing forests with agricultural land for both crops and livestock, logging for wood, the collection of fuel wood, and the construction of housing and roads.

The earth's population today is 6.7 billion. Between 1960 and 1999, the population doubled from 3 billion to 6 billion people. This population increase reflects the fact that people are now healthier and better nourished than at any other time in history. However, it also has intensified the impact of deforestation, pollution, the depletion of resources, and other global environmental issues.

People are buying and using more products than at any other time in history. According to the World Rainforest Movement, "overconsumption by consumers in high-income countries constitutes another of the major underlying causes of deforestation."

With possible high profits to be made from consumer products, forests are routinely cleared for large-scale agriculture or cattle-raising operations. One example is the rise in popularity of the fast-food hamburger, which has required huge quantities of cheap meat and has resulted in widespread deforestation in Central America and Brazil for cattle ranching. Similarly, paper consumption has skyrocketed in high-income countries, resulting in a high need for cheap wood to make it. "Forests are thus being cleared in Indonesia—and many other parts of the world—to give way to eucalyptus plantations aimed at supplying that market with increasing amounts of cheap raw material."

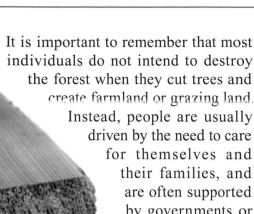

It is important to remember that most individuals do not intend to destroy the forest when they cut trees and create farmland or grazing land. Instead, people are usually driven by the need to care for themselves and their families, and are often supported by governments or corporations that may build roads allowing access or offer land and other incentives, and by consumers who buy the goods they produce. But individual actions can cause a global problem when they are repeated by many different people in many different places.

One direct consequence of the rising population is more people to feed. Since 1970, the Earth's cultivated farmland has more than quadrupled in area, from more than 1 million square miles in 1970 to more than 5 million square miles in 2000.

In fact, the single largest direct cause of deforestation today is the conversion of forests to agricultural land. People are cutting and clearing forestland and turning it into farmland or ranchland worldwide. However, most of the deforested land is not used by farmers to feed their families or even the local people. Rather, most of it is used to produce crops like coffee, cacao, and soybeans, or with cattle or other livestock—all aimed for sale to high-income countries. Thus, the rises of both consumption and population growth are factors in forests being converted to agricultural lands.

In the Amazon region of Brazil, for example, nearly 80 percent of the land deforested from 1996 to 2006 is now used for cattle pasture. During that time period, more than 38,600 square miles—an area the size of Ireland—was cleared for cattle ranching as Brazil rose to become the world's largest beef exporter. Cattle-ranching has grown almost five-fold since the 1970s. The deforestation is likely to continue as the Brazilian government is reported to be offering low-interest loans and other incentives to beef producers.

A cash crop is a plant farmed specifically for sale rather than to feed and sustain the farmer's family. Cash crops like coffee, cocoa, oil palm, and bananas are another significant cause of

deforestation and, like animal grazing, are directly tied to consumption. "Since the early 1970s, the area devoted to oil palm, cocoa, and coffee in developing countries has doubled from 500,000 to 1 million square kilometers [193,000 to 386,000 square miles]," according to David Perry. "That is an area three times the size of Germany. Much of this growth came at the expense of forests." With coffee growing, for example, the deforestation has meant critical loss of native habitat. According to Conservation International, three-quarters of the twenty-five "biodiversity hotspots" it has identified are in major coffee growing areas.

The United Nations predicts that in some areas of the world, particularly in South America, high food prices will continue to favor clearing the forest to produce cash crops, meaning that deforestation will persist.

Another cause of deforestation is logging, where people cut trees to sell for paper, building materials, furniture, and other wood-based products. Like the conversion of forests to agricultural land, logging is driven by rises in both population and consumption.

It used to be that almost all logging was done in natural forests. However, many countries today practice plantation forestry, where trees are planted and grown like a crop and logged when they are mature, and then the area is replanted to grow new trees. Still, in numerous areas of the world, logging of natural forests continues to be practiced and often leads to deforestation. In the 1990s, logging companies began operations in Siberia, causing a tremendous amount of deforestation there.

Logging is especially problematic in tropical areas. As one reporter describes it, "Despite improved logging techniques and greater international awareness and concern for the rain forests, unsustainable logging of tropical rain forests continues—much of it practiced illegally by criminal syndicates." Logging operations in these areas are often focused on short-term profits, with little incentive to consider the long-term consequences. Because tropical rain forests typically have a mix of many different types of trees, it is often cheaper for loggers to cut down the entire forest rather than selectively log the trees they want. Even when selective logging is practiced, the forest can be destroyed because logging a single large tree can also bring down dozens of trees connected to it by a network of vines.

People using wood for food is another direct cause of deforestation. In many parts of the world, people still do their daily cooking and heating completely with firewood or fuelwood.

Millions of people collect or cut fuelwood in the forested areas around their homes and villages, or must buy it from others who have collected it. As the human population in these areas expands, fuelwood need grows proportionately. As Alain Marcoux, a senior officer with the UN's Food and Agriculture Organization, describes, "When the annual use of wood exceeds the sustainable yield of wooded areas, forests and woodlands are gradually destroyed. In some dry areas such as the West African Sahel, fuelwood collection is by far the dominant factor of deforestation."

Wood Energy

What is the source of energy you use to cook or heat your home? Natural gas or electricity is the most likely answer in the United States. In Africa the story is different. Wood-fuel provides 58 percent of all the energy used on the continent of Africa and 90 percent of the wood collected or harvested is used for energy. Wood-fuel remains the most important source of energy for more than 2 billion people across the globe, mostly in developing countries. Most of that energy use is for cooking and heating. In forty developing countries, wood-fuel provides more than 70 percent of all energy use.

In the past decade, developed countries that are encouraging the use of renewable energy have also turned to wood-fuels. The high prices of fossil fuels have turned more countries to wood as an ingredient for their countries' renewable sources of energy. The International Energy Agency indicates that renewable energy sources will continue to increase. Cooking and heating will remain the principal uses for wood-fuel in developing countries, and the use of biofuels for the production of electricity is expected to triple by 2030. ■

Another important cause of deforestation is the conversion of forests to houses, cities, and towns. As the global population rises, so does the need for housing and services. In the eastern United States, for example, forests are being lost to suburban development at a growing rate. Not only is the population expanding, but an increased standard of living in the region has led individuals to seek larger houses and properties than before, compounding the loss.

Throughout the world, deforestation is often initiated by the construction of roads. When a road is built through a natural forest, it allows access to loggers, farmers, and hunters in the forest areas, typically accelerating the forest's decline.

Wildfires, hurricanes, volcanoes, landslides, and other natural events can cause a loss of forest as well. Wildfires can be particularly devastating. In the 1990s, for example, 111 million acres in Russia alone were burned by wildfires. These disturbances are usually temporary and, given time, the forest will recover from these events.

Deforestation has both environmental and social impacts. Some of these are confined to the area where the deforestation occurs, but many can ripple throughout the region and even the world.

Forests contain more than half of all the species living on our planet. With deforestation, many of the plants and animals in the region face extinction, a problem that is particularly acute in the tropics. One example of species loss due to deforestation is in Singapore, where more than 95 percent of the original forest has been cleared since 1819. An astounding 73 percent of the species in Singapore—birds, butterflies, fish, mammals, and more—have gone extinct since that time.

A loss of species means a loss of diversity within the remaining ecosystem. Deforestation destroys an environment that has existed and evolved over millions of years, and we do not know the full consequences of diversity loss for that environment or for the world.

Forests are intricately linked with the water cycle and deforestation can adversely affect that cycle, both locally and beyond. In the Amazon basin, for example, forests seem to "rake" water from clouds that come through the canopy, causing more rain to fall in the area. When the forest is removed, the region doesn't get as much rainfall. In fact, some tropical areas (especially in Asia and the Pacific) have seen long-term declines in rainfall in the twentieth century, a period of heavy deforestation.

In both Costa Rica and Puerto Rico, a loss of forest in lowland areas has been linked to changes in climate and reduced cloud cover in mountain forests, an indication that large-scale deforestation can affect climate across broad regions.

The Domino Effect of Deforestation

A forest is more than a cluster of trees. It is a set of complex interactions that affect the soil, temperatures, and the cycling of water, which in turn affect all the plants and animals living in the area. When an area of forest is cut down or degraded, various changes trigger other changes, in a cascading domino effect. For example, when trees are removed, the soil is exposed to more sun. The lack of a tree canopy causes moisture to evaporate more quickly. Soils become dry and cracked.

Trees help to stabilize temperatures by providing shade. With deforestation, the temperatures become more extreme so that they are hotter in the day and cooler at night. In a tropical rain forest, for example, temperatures may be 60° F at night and up to 98° F in the day; once deforested they may be as low as 45° F at night and up to 130° F in the day. Forest trees also help hold soil in place with their roots and the dead leaf matter on the soil surface. The tree canopy protects the soil from the full force of rain. With deforestation, rain hits the soil directly, causing the nutrient-rich layer to wash away.

Forests help to cycle water within an area by allowing rainwater to soak into the ground, holding water in their leaves, which then evaporates locally, increasing rainfall in the area. With deforestation, rain runs off rather than soaking into the ground and moisture in the air moves to other locations. When tropical areas are deforested, soils dry and erosion increases. Over time, these conditions will lead to the area becoming like a desert with few things able to grow. ■

Deforestation impacts our global climate as well. It is estimated that deforestation is responsible for one-fifth of the global total of human-caused carbon emissions every year, contributing almost as much to climate change as the use of fossil fuels in the United States.

Another impact of deforestation is a process known as desertification. This is when an ecosystem is degraded to the point that soils are continually dry and few plants are able to grow. Desertification affects the livelihoods of millions of people worldwide, and threatens the world's poorest populations. Studies have shown that destruction of rain forests in West African countries like Nigeria, Ghana, and Côte d'Ivoire may have caused two decades of droughts in the interior of Africa, leading to widespread hardship and famine.

A crop of corn (also known in some countries as maize) suffers from drought in Tanzania, a country in East Africa.

The Power of Fire

In late August 2009, a fire in Angeles National Forest in California destroyed more than 100,000 acres of dense forests, underbrush, and scrub oak. The fire also claimed the lives of two fire fighters, forced the closing of numerous schools, destroyed sixty-two homes, and reduced the air quality in the area to hazardous levels. North of Los Angeles, during the same time period, a 4,600-acre fire burned in Yosemite National Park, and in the mountains southwest of San Jose yet another fire burned, destroying 2,600 acres of brush and timber, and forcing the evacuation of at least 2,000 people.

A world away in Greece, also in August of 2009, a huge wildfire sent tens of thousands of people fleeing from their

homes. The flames seared about 37,000 acres of land, including some of the last forests near the capital city of Athens. "A significant part of the forest has been lost," lamented Constantinos Liarikos, the conservation director for the World Wildlife Fund in Greece. "The fire will surely affect the Athens region's microclimate."

Globally, forest fires are not a new phenomenon. They occur naturally, set off by lightning, a volcanic eruption, or spontaneous combustion of dry sawdust and leaves. But in most instances fire is the result of human actions, such as carelessness or negligence—tossing a lit cigarette stub or match into dry, dense bush can lead to a wildfire. Historically, people

have used fire to clear forests for agricultural activities, in the U.S. and worldwide. And then there are fires that have been set intentionally by arsonists, some of whom profit from such acts.

Fires can be helpful as well as harmful. On the one hand, they play a natural and important role in the life-cycle of a forest. Forest fires clear out old brush, so that new growth can emerge. And even after the most destructive fire, life remains. Though above ground a tree may appear dead, its roots often survive, as do its seeds. Sometimes the seeds have scattered in the brush or have been buried underground. In fact, the seeds of a western shrub called buckbrush, which is found in numbers of western parks, can remain dormant for hundreds of years. They germinate only when they're subjected to the heat of a fire. Animals also manage to adapt to the harsh conditions left in the wake of a wildfire.

"A lot of insects, rodents and even amphibians can survive the passing of a flame front," says Timothy Ingalsbee, executive director of the Western Fire Ecology Center for the American Lands Alliance, and a former fire fighter with the U.S. Forest Service and the National Park Service in the 1980s. "Small animals like rodents will often burrow underground [until the fire has passed], or climb inside downed logs.

"People usually do not perceive a forest that has just been burned as beautiful," the Western Fire Ecology Center explains in its literature on fire ecology. "But fire is a part of the natural world, just like the wind, the rain, and other natural forces. Wildfires are an essential feature of ecosystems; both plants and animals are well adapted to fires and benefit from fire. Fire is an agent of change, performing a variety of functions and producing a range of effects."

Still, it can take decades, or hundreds of years, for a forest to reach maturity after the ravages of a catastrophic wildfire. The destruction caused by forest fires also leads to serious social and economic consequences. In 1997 and 1998, millions of acres of forests around the world caught fire during an intense El Nino-related drought. In Indonesia, as many as 75 million people were adversely affected by the hot, fast-moving fires of 1997-98. Some 40,000 had to be hospitalized for respiratory ailments, such as asthma, and the total cost of the fires was estimated at $9.3 billion, according to the World Wildlife Fund.

In the U.S., in 2008, there were 78,979 wildfires, burning 5.2 million acres. And that was down from the previous year, when 85,705 fires burned 9.3 million acres. In the coming decades, scientists expect wildfires to increase as the climate warms. ■

Chapter Three
U.S. Forests:
Changes Over Time

The Pilgrims sent the ship *Fortune* back to England in 1592 "laden with good clapboard." It was the first of thousands of ships that would be sent to Europe with logs and lumber to meet the needs of the European builders. There was a great demand in Europe for wood because of the deforestation that had already occurred in that region. Wood was also being consumed in staggering quantities in the developing country that was to become the United States of America. Wood was the building material of choice and was also the major source of fuel.

Travelers to the New World were awestruck by the abundance and diversity of trees they found. In 1637, Thomas Morton, in his *New English Canaan*, wrote:

> Oakes . . . of two sorts, white and redd; excellent tymber for building both of howses and shipping . . . Ashe . . . very good for staves, oares or pikes. . . Elme, . . . Beech . . . of two sorts, redd and white; very excellent for trenchers or chairs . . . . Wallnutt . . . an excellent wood, for many uses approoved.

Morton also named pine, cedar, cypress, spruce, alder, birch, maple, hawthorn, and many more.

Between 1600 and 1810 European settlers cut and cleared the forests along the 1,800 miles of coast from northern Florida to northern Maine for farming and the grazing of livestock, for fuel, the construction of houses, mills, barns, warehouses, fences, and furniture, and for semi-industrial and commercial use. As one historian put it, "[wood] entered into every aspect of life, quite literally from cradle to coffin."

In 1831, Alexis de Tocqueville spent 271 days traveling to seventeen states in America. The French aristocrat, then age twenty-five, observed the rapid thinning of the forests and wrote:

> [He] fells the forests and drains the marshes . . . . The wilds become villages, and the villages towns. The American, the daily witness of such wonders, does not see anything astonishing in all this. This incredible destruction, this even more surprising growth, seems to him the usual progress of things in this world. He gets accustomed to it as to the unalterable order of nature.

Change in the North American forest had started even before the first European settlers arrived in the late sixteenth century. Today, historians and scientists widely believe that the American Indian populations altered the forest and impacted other natural resources. The Indians had been in the Americas for millennia. They had been cutting, clearing, and burning the forests for agriculture and hunting, and also to remove cover for potential enemies, to clear the way for travel on horseback, and to reduce insect pests.

From Maine to the Gulf, nearly all Indians lived in fixed villages, surrounded by fields, where they grew maize, kidney beans, potatoes, squash, sweet potatoes, tobacco, watermelons, and sunflowers. John Smith described the villages of the Pawhatans: "Their houses are in the midst of their fields or gardens, which are small plots of ground. Some 20 acres, some 40, some 100, some 200, some more, some less. In some places from 20 to 50 of those houses together or but little separated by groves of trees. Near their habitations is little wood or old trees on the ground by reason of them burning of them by fire. So that a man may gallop a horse amongst the woods any way."

Though the Indians had altered the forests, their impact was nothing compared to what had been done in Europe or would soon to be started by the European colonists in the Americas. America was about to experience deforestation.

Near the beginning of European settlement in 1630, the original American forest covered nearly 1.6 million square miles, or about half of the U.S. land area (including Alaska). For the settlers the forest provided both a challenge and opportunity. Early in the settlement process, the forest prevented expansion and growth of the communities. The forest needed to be cut and converted to agricultural land. Later, the colonists increasingly used the forest resources for a source of building materials for home, fences, business, and especially ships. The first sawmill in America was in York, Maine, in 1623. By 1645 the best and straightest trees were being reserved for the British Royal Navy. The forests of the region had become a

The HMS *Victory* is the only surviving warship of Britain's Royal Navy from the mid-eighteenth century. Launched in 1765, it continued in active service for the next thirty-four years, and today is a museum ship in Portsmouth, England.

source of employment and income for settlers and communities. The best timber trees—usually white pine, oak, and chestnut—were the first to be cut. Most of these would be sawed and used in construction of the growing communities.

As the population grew in the 1700s agriculture expanded and more land was needed to provide the growing demand for food. Since the forests seemed endless, little thought went into conserving the resources.

Most Americans (95 percent) were subsistence farmers in 1800, and they needed the forest cleared to grow food. They needed fences, too. Instead of herding livestock, the settlers let their hogs, cattle, and other livestock roam untended into the woods. The fences were needed to keep the animals out of fields and gardens. Douglas W. MacCleery, an assistant director with the U.S. Forest Service and author of *American Forest: A History of Resiliency and Recovery*, wrote that "in 1850, there were 3.2 million miles of wood fences in the United States—enough to circle the earth over 120 times."

Between 1810 and 1865, America began to transition from a rural-agricultural society to an urban-industrial society. With this transition came an even greater need for wood—for steam engines for riverboats and railways. According to MacCleery, "in 1840, almost 900,000 cords of wood were sold for steamboat fuel, or a fifth of all fuelwood sold."

By the mid-1800s, America was one of the largest countries in the world, and railroads linked the nation's growing cities. "Except for the engine and rails, railroads were made of wood," MacCleery explained. "The cars were wood, the ties were wood, the fuel was wood, the bridges and trestles were wood and the station houses, fences and telegraph poles were wood. The mileage of U.S. Railroads increased more than 35 times between 1850 and 1910. By the late 1800s, railroads accounted for between 20-25 percent of the total consumption of timber in the country."

Continued growth in population and the westward expansion led people to the great forests of the Midwest. In the

A Washington logging train hauls a fir tree 12 feet in diameter down a mountain in this 1908 photo.

mid-1800s logging crews had gone to the Great Lakes region to meet the growing demand for lumber and wood products to supply the growing population and the westward expansion. Wood in 1850 accounted for 90 percent of America's growing energy consumption. Deforestation rates at their peak in the Midwest were approximately 2 percent annually, about the rates now seen in the Amazon. As the Rev. Frederick Starr of St. Louis observed, the nation's growth and prosperity depended upon "cheap bread, cheap house, cheap fuel and cheap transportation for passengers and freight," and wood figured prominently in these "four great departments of industry and living."

The better soils of the Midwest also shifted agriculture to this region, causing the abandonment of some of the early agricultural lands in New England. This land would revert back to forest over the next generations.

There was no national effort to manage or conserve the American forest until the 1850s. The movement of change toward conservation and protection had its beginnings when

In this 1906 photo three men sit amidst a forest devastated by logging in the Cascade Mountains, near Seattle, Washington.

great writers began to celebrate the values of nature and the forests in their writings. Henry David Thoreau was one of the first, supporting the idea that nature was one with God and must be preserved. Other great writers like Ralph Waldo Emerson and James Fennimore Cooper supported similar views.

Reverend Starr was also an early advocate for the preservation of the country's forests. In 1865, he wrote an article titled "American Forests: Their Destruction and Preservation," which appeared in the *Annual Report* of the commissioner of agriculture. In the article, he said: "There are few subjects so closely connected with the wants of society, the general health of the people, the salubrity of the climate, the production of our soils, and the increase of our national wealth, as our forests; and yet no considerable interest of our country has received so little attention at the hands of the people, and enjoyed so little fostering protection from the government."

After the Civil War, the need for a forest conservation movement had gained momentum with the public. The predecessor to the U.S. Forest Service had its origin in 1876, just four years after the first national park, Yellowstone, had been established. The first national forests were designated in 1891 in Colorado and Wyoming. They encompassed nearly 2.5 million acres. Gifford Pinchot was named chief of the Division of Forestry in 1898, and with President Theodore Roosevelt saw the growth of the U.S. Forest Service, both in importance and size.

Pinchot, perhaps more than any other individual, is associated with the idea of efficient forest management to meet the needs of people. It was Pinchot who announced a land management policy that sought to develop wisely all natural resources for "the greatest good of the greatest number for the longest time." The principle of conservation—managing the land and its resources for multiple uses on a sustainable basis—has guided the United States Forest Service since the agency's creation in 1905. Soon, under the aggressive support of President Roosevelt, another 100 million acres had been added to the U.S. National Forests.

During the same years, a German-born teacher and forester, Carl Alwen Schenck, brought his skills and training to the United States in the late 1800s. He was to be the chief forester for the George Vanderbilt Biltmore estate property in North Carolina. This appointment would eventually lead to the establishment of the first American School of Forestry that would be moved later to Yale University.

Still, the forest was being cut over. The low point in the amount of forest cover in the United States was around 1920 when only about 1 million square miles of forests remained. Nearly 40 percent of the U.S. forests had been cut, with many areas being converted to agriculture or rapidly growing urban areas.

During the early 1900s, forest areas in the United States started to reclaim some of the land. The forest cover was increasing, largely through abandonment of cropland and regrowth on harvested areas primarily in the East. Some states saw significant regrowth of trees or development of

A 1909 photo of Gifford Pinchot, the first chief of the U.S. Forest Service.

what would be called secondary forests. In Vermont, forest cover has more than doubled—from 37 percent in 1850 to 77 percent today. In New Hampshire, forest cover was 50 percent in 1850 compared to 87 percent today. Maine, where the first saw mill was built, reached a low of 53 percent in 1872 and today is the highest percentage of all states at 90 percent.

Today, 33 percent (1.1 million square miles) of the total land area in the United States is forested, a reduction of 13 percent from 1630 when 46 percent of the area was forested. But this figure of 33 percent is up 7 percent from the lowest percentage found in 1920.

Since the 1600s, 90 percent of the original primary forests that covered much of the contiguous forty-eight states had been cleared. Forest area in the United States, however, has remained relatively stable, but it changes in both regional and species composition. In the East, reversion of marginal farmland to forest has been common. In the South, large-scale planting of pine trees has taken the place of farmland. Another dimension of growth has been attributed to successful fire control. These gains in forest land have been at a higher rate than the loss of forest for current new development and natural disasters.

The amount of protective forest in the United States has continued to rise since the late 1800s, with the initial national parks and national forests. There are 266 million acres of protected forests today in the United States, mostly in national and state parks, and in designated wilderness areas. Unlike most countries, a high percentage of the forests in the United States are privately owned. According to the American Forest Foundation, "Almost 60 percent of our nation's forests are privately owned. A program of the American Forest Foundation, the American Tree Farm System, provides these forest owners with the technical, training, and education to ensure the long-term sustainability of our nations' private forests."

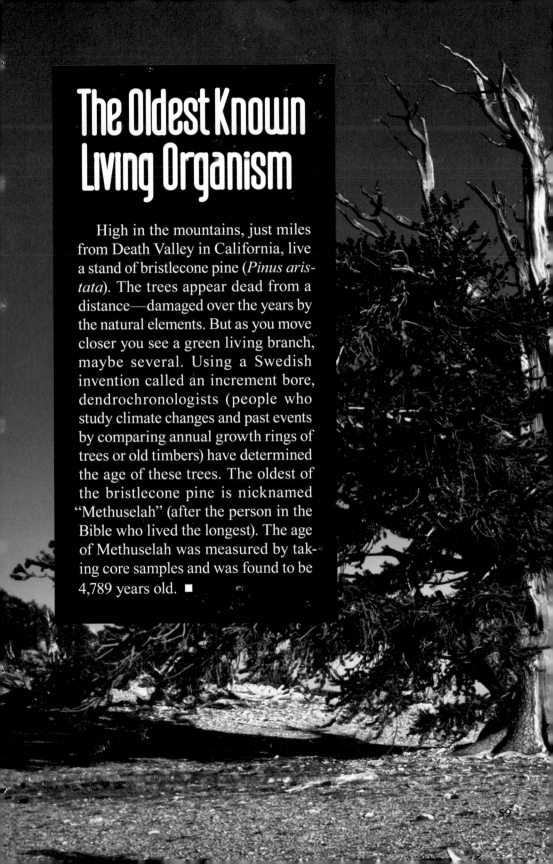

The Oldest Known Living Organism

High in the mountains, just miles from Death Valley in California, live a stand of bristlecone pine (*Pinus aristata*). The trees appear dead from a distance—damaged over the years by the natural elements. But as you move closer you see a green living branch, maybe several. Using a Swedish invention called an increment bore, dendrochronologists (people who study climate changes and past events by comparing annual growth rings of trees or old timbers) have determined the age of these trees. The oldest of the bristlecone pine is nicknamed "Methuselah" (after the person in the Bible who lived the longest). The age of Methuselah was measured by taking core samples and was found to be 4,789 years old. ∎

World's Tallest Tree

Growing in a temperate forest in California is the world's tallest known tree. In September 2006, Jim Spickler, a tree canopy scientist, was part of an expedition to climb the world's tallest tree, named "Hyperion." The giant sequoia (*Sequoia sempervirens*) is as tall as a thirty-five story building. Famous naturalist John Muir wrote about climbing the majestic trees of California. While at the top of a one-hundred-foot Douglas fir, he wrote "never before did I enjoy so noble an exhilaration of motion. The slender tops fairly flapped and swished in the passionate torrent, bending and swirling backward and forward, round and round, tracing indescribable combinations of vertical and horizontal curves, while I clung with muscles firm braced, like a bobo-link on a reed." ∎

Chapter Four
Amazonia: Deforestation of a Global Forest

It is called Amazonia, the watershed of the Amazon and its many tributaries. Amazonia is the largest tract of primary forest in the world. The Amazon River Basin was once—not that many years ago—an undisturbed and inaccessible region of the earth. Today, that is changing. Population growth, highway construction, forest fires, the invasion of exotic species, economic development, the extraction of nontimber resources, and the practice of selective logging (legal

or illegal) of valuable species like mahogany are threatening the integrity of the Amazonian forests. In parts of the Amazon, the building of hydroelectric dams also impact the forests, causing flooding of extensive areas of forest.

The Amazonian forest is considered by many scientists to be one of the planet's most important natural ecosystems. Consider the following facts and figures to gain an idea of the significance of this global wonder:

- The size of the Amazon basin is 2.7 million square miles—an area covering about three-fourths of the United States.
- The Amazonian forest represents more than 50 percent of the world's tropical forests.
- It totals 6 percent of the total land surface of the planet, but hosts an estimated 50 percent of the world's species, with millions of species still to be discovered.
- More than 500 species of trees have been found in just 2.5 acres and about half of the world's species of trees are found in the Amazon. With this volume of trees, only about 2 percent of the sunlight reaches the floor of the forest.
- Spreads across parts of eight counties: Brazil (68 percent), Bolivia (10 percent), Peru (9 percent), Colombia (6 percent), Guyana (3 percent), Surinam (2 percent), Ecuador (2 percent), and Venezuela (1 percent).
- The volume of water captured by the Amazon basin each year is 20 percent of the earth's surface freshwater. Fifty percent of all rainfall returns to the atmosphere by transpiration in the forest.

The forests of Amazonia are home to an enormous variety of flora and fauna, which contain a genetic reservoir unsur-

passed on the globe. The Amazon forest canopy is also a key component of the global carbon cycle.

Carbon dioxide, or CO_2, is a major contributor to the greenhouse effect and to global climate change. Trees take up CO_2 from the atmosphere and use it to make the glucose or sugars that make up the tree. As long as the trees are alive and growing, they store this carbon. But when forests are cleared and the trees either burned or left to decay, this carbon is released

back into the atmosphere. It is estimated that deforestation is responsible for one-fifth of the global total of carbon emissions every year, contributing almost as much to climate change as the use of fossil fuels in the U.S.

The lush canopy of Amazonia takes in CO_2 in the process of photosynthesis and then exhales oxygen, thereby providing a carbon sink that removes millions of tons of greenhouse gases each year from our atmosphere. But the Amazon can

also be a source of CO_2 for the earth's atmosphere, through deforestation, respiration, and decomposition. Because of this, the Amazon is a global climate regulator.

During the past forty years, close to 20 percent of the Amazon rain forest has been cut—more than in all the previous 450 years since European colonization began. Changes in the Amazon affect not only the regional environment but have a significant impact on the earth's systems.

There are many competing economic forces that want to claim the natural resources of the region. Much of the land has been reserved for the indigenous peoples who have lived on the land for generations.

Two men armed with saws cut into a large tree in Brazilian rain forest.

72

Inset photo: An aerial view of deforestation of rain forests in Brazil near the Amazon River.

Millions of poor Brazilians also want to begin farming and calling land their own. The population living in the basin in 2007 was estimated to be 33.5 million—an increase from the 5 million that lived there in the early 1970s.

Cattle-herding also impacts the region. Brazil has the world's largest cattle herd, requiring both range and food. Then there are the large agribusinesses wanting to move into the area. These businesses generate revenue for the country and are considered desirable by the Brazilian government, because the government needs ways to pay off its international debt.

Fire is yet another factor. Fire is relatively new to Amazonia, an area that before widespread human settlement had not experienced a "fire season." The slash and burn technique has been used for years as a tool for clearing forest and converting it to agricultural land. But these intentional fires can expand or get "away" from people and burn into the remaining forested regions that they border. "The first accidental burn that steals into the forest is the beginning of a long, downward spiral that compromises forest health over an area equal to or greater than the amount that is deforested outright each year," stated Daniel

C. Nepstad, a senior scientist and tropical forest ecologist with Woods Hole Research Center in Massachusetts.

During the last half of the twentieth century one of the most significant ecological transformations in the Amazonian region has been the short lapse of time between forest fires. Instead of centuries between events, some fires are now burning with lapses of five to fifteen years. Concentrations of fire or hot spots areas are also closely associated with road-building areas. From 2003 to 2006 there were, on average, 24,000 hot spots per year in the Amazon—mostly in Brazil.

While fire clears the land for agriculture, the infertile soil that remains is not suited for successful farming. The initial surge of nutrients from the ash is quickly used by the crops, and in a matter of several years the soil becomes infertile and cannot support intensive agriculture. Since most of the farmers do not have the incomes required to purchase soil additives and fertilizers, the land is only used for a few years. When the soils are depleted, the farmer moves on to a new piece of deforested land.

There are different types of agricultural activities in Amazonia. Some agricultural areas are dedicated to

self-sufficient crops, mainly cassava, maize, rice, beans, bananas, and different native or introduced fruits, while agro-industrial crop areas grow large areas of African oil palms, cocoa, annatto, fibers, tea, coffee, and others. More recently, the consolidation of the complex grains (soya, rice, sunflower, sorghum, and maize), is rapidly expanding the agricultural frontier towards the interior of Amazonia.

The expansion of soya cultivation, in particular, is a response to the growing international market demand and the availability of relatively low-cost land. Eric Jackson, chief editor of the *Panama News*, an English-language newspaper in Panama, wrote that "the soybean farmers are a relatively new but important factor in deforestation, and not only because they directly and indirectly clear vast tracts. Because of their political and economic power they are in a position to resist government policies designed to restrain deforestation. They also tend to find support when they advocate new roads through the forest to get their produce to world markets."

Illegal logging is also a problem in the forests, and it has economic, social, and environmental repercussions. Illegal logging upsets the market by providing an oversupply of cheap but illegally harvested wood. This prevents law-abiding operators in the region from investing in sustainable forestry practices and best management practices when harvesting the timber.

Brazilian environmental police are attempting to curb illegal logging and are having some success. In April 2009, they seized the equivalent of 400 truckloads of wood in a major raid on illegal loggers in an area east of Belem City. The Environment Minister Carlos Minc stated the goals of his agency: "We are determined to slash deforestation—the operation is a warning to illegal loggers." Minc also said that "alternative economic solutions" are needed to provide support for the people living in the region.

Education will be one of the critical foundations for success in preserving Amazonia. The knowledge of how the Amazonia

A barge loaded with logs on Marajó, the world's largest marine-fluvial island. Located in the Amazon delta between the Amazon and Pará Rivers, the island is the size of Switzerland, and its western half is covered with primary forests.

region really works is still very limited. More research and data collections are needed to understand how this complex system works and how to predict with any success what will happen in the future. An educated citizenry, both global and local, is critical for understanding the challenges and for taking action. Local education is moving in the right direction, but still remains low. There has been an increase in the number of years children spend in school, from an average of 4.1 years in 1990 to 5.9 years in 2005. In addition, the participation of children from seven to fourteen years in basic education improved from 85 percent in 1990 to 96 percent in 2005.

In the report "Environmental Outlook in the Amazonia: GEO Amazonia," United Nations Under-Secretary General Achim Steiner and Acting Secretary General Francisco J. Ruiz M. state that "While Amazonia has suffered many environmental hazards, we remain convinced that the region's leaders will make the right decisions to halt environmental degradation and promote sustainable development for the good of the region's inhabitants and for all of humanity."

Indigenous Peoples

Around the year 1500, the land we now call Brazil once had a population that numbered in the millions. Some estimates by demographers had about 2.4 million people; other estimates went as high as 5 million. The early European visitors brought with them diseases like smallpox, typhoid, dysentery, and influenza—diseases that decimated the populations of the indigenous tribes.

For centuries, the rain forest acted as a natural barrier, with its difficult navigation, against European settlers and the diseases they might spread. Some isolated indigenous peoples lived, and still live, in places that are almost impossible to reach, and they subsist by taking advantage of the forest's resources.

Today, there are 420 different indigenous peoples living in Amazonia who speak eighty-six languages and 650 dialects. "The indigenous people knew thousands of vegetable species and they used them for many different purposes," according to Mark Plotkin, an ethnobotanist and president of the nonprofit group Amazon Conservation Team (ACT). "They collected fruits and seeds, used the bejucos (climbing plants) and the lianas (long-stemmed, usually woody vines) to build their dwellings and basic utensils; large tree trunks to make canoes and rafts, palm leaves to protect themselves from inclement weather; as well as magic-medicinal species."

ACT is working with indigenous populations and other conservation groups to support what Plotkin has termed "bio-cultural conservation."

"It's our strong belief that the people who best know, use, and protect biodiversity are the indigenous people who live in these forests," Plotkin explains. "The best way to protect ancestral rainforests is to help the Indians hold on to their cul-

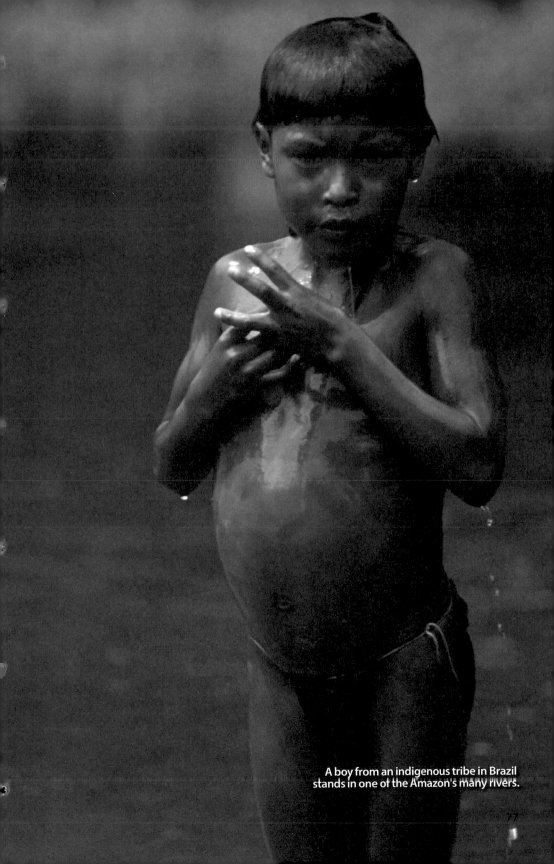

A boy from an indigenous tribe in Brazil stands in one of the Amazon's many rivers.

ture, and the best way to help them hold onto their culture is to help them protect the rainforest."

Barbara Zimmerman with Conservation International said "indigenous territories have proved formidable barriers to forest destruction in the southeastern Amazon. These indigenous territories comprise some 35 million acres (14 million hectares) controlled by approximately 7,000 Kayapó Indians and another 5,500 Indians from 14 ethnic groups."

However, Zimmerman adds that pressure from outside development continues to intensify. "Indigenous territories . . . constantly risk invasion by ranchers, colonists, fraudulent land developers, commercial fishermen, loggers, and gold-miners. . . . Without additional support the future of the indigenous populations is very uncertain." ■

Chapter Five
The Disappearing Mangroves: The Tidal Forest

O n December 26, 2004, one of the world's worst natural disasters occurred when an earthquake under
the Indian Ocean generated the biggest tsunami the
world had seen in at least forty years. Waves as high as 32 feet
pounded the coastlines of thirteen countries in Asia and Africa.
More than 220,000 people perished. Millions more were dis-
placed and left destitute, and thousands of homes, roads, and
other infrastructures were destroyed. The earthquake was

the fourth-largest in the world since 1900, and the waves it triggered were estimated to have released the power of atom bombs—like that which hit Hiroshima.

In the days, weeks, and months after the disaster, stories began to emerge from survivors, scientists, and environmentalists who reported that in some cases mangrove forests had saved lives and property. Fishermen told of how they took shelter in mangroves. Locals reported that the mangroves broke the impact of the waves and prevented people from being washed out to sea. A CNN story told of a baby boy in Thailand who was saved by the mangroves when the water rushed in and out without destroying everything in its path. Selvam Vaithilingam of the MS Swaminathan Research Foundation in Madras, India, said 172 families in a fishing village in India's Tamil Naidu state survived only because the mangroves are thriving and dense there. They decreased the level of inundation by breaking the height and the velocity of the waves.

"The tsunami left a horrific human tragedy in its wake but also some lessons," said Faizal Parish, director of the Global Environment Centre in Malaysia. "Among them is the tremendous importance of mangroves, which are one of the world's most threatened tropical ecosystems."

A mangrove is a salt-tolerant tree or shrub that has tangled roots that grow above ground. Mangroves are unique forests found along the sheltered coastlines, lagoons, estuaries, rivers, and deltas of 120 coastal countries—most close to the equator, but one group goes as far south as New Zealand. The species of mangroves will vary according to the climate, salinity of the water, and the topography of the area they are growing in.

The term "mangrove" describes both the ecosystem and the types of plant families that live in a tidal environment. They are very diverse—they include about seventy species

This photo shows damage from the December 26, 2004, tsunami in the Indian state of Tamil Nadu.

of plants that range in size from small shrub species to trees that can reach 131 feet in height. Large stretches of mangroves border the coastal areas of Asia, Africa, Oceania, and the Americas. In Florida, for example, there are three species of mangroves: red mangrove (*Rhizophora mangle*), black mangrove (*Avicennia germinans*), and white mangrove (*Luguncularia racemosa*).

The countries with the largest areas of mangroves are Indonesia, Brazil, Australia, Nigeria, and Mexico. The mangroves in these countries represent 64 percent of the world's

mangroves. The largest remaining tract of mangrove forest in the world is found along the edge of the Bay of Bengal, which stretches from Bangladesh to India. The area is called the Sundarbans, meaning "beautiful forest." This area is one of the few regions of the world where the Bengal tiger can still be found.

Mangroves have a filter system to keep the salt levels low. Up top they have salt-excreting leaves and below a complex root system consisting of aerial and salt-filtering roots that allow them to survive and thrive in the coastal areas. The expansive root system also helps to trap sediment coming off the land and prevent it from reaching out into the ocean. This has the added value of protecting coral reefs from being covered with sediment and also prevents the sedimentation of shipping lanes. Queensland's mangroves along the coast of Australia do much to sustain the Great Barrier Reef, the world's largest coral reef system.

Scientists and environmentalists are just beginning to fully understand the importance of mangrove forests. Many believe that mangrove forests are essential in the protection of coastal areas from natural disasters like cyclones, hurricanes, floods, and tsunamis. But others disagree; they argue that there is no evidence to support the idea that mangroves act as "bioshields."

Still others are adamant that mangrove forests provide a buffer from tsunamis and storms, and their removal in

regions around the world has resulted in repeated tragedies. "Encroachment into mangrove forests, which used to serve as a buffer between the rising tide, between big waves and storms and residential areas; all those lands have been destroyed," states Surin Pitsuwan, secretary-general of the Association of South-East Asian Nations. "Human beings are now the direct victims of such natural forces."

Mangroves also play an important role in the marine food system. They support biodiversity by providing habitat, spawning and nursery grounds, and nutrients for many species of fish and shellfish that inhabit the entangling roots. Birds benefit from the forests, too, and in Florida, a number of threatened and endangered species, such as the American Crocodile and Atlantic Saltmarsh Snake, make use of the mangrove habitats.

But mangroves are under constant threat. They are impacted by the increased population of people in coastal areas; the clearing of land for coastal development; agriculture; mining; tourism; and the harvesting of wood for houses, fuel, furniture, boats, fence posts, charcoal, and even traditional medicines.

The most comprehensive study of this ecosystem shows that the current mangrove area worldwide has fallen from 46.5 million acres in 1980 to 37.5 million acres in 2005. "The World's Mangroves 1980-2005" was prepared by the United Nation's Food and Agriculture Organization (FAO) and mangrove specialists from around the world. The study found the world has lost 9 million acres over the last twenty-five years, or 20 percent of those found in 1980. The current annual loss is almost 2 percent per year. The FAO estimates that mangroves are critically endangered or approaching extinction in twenty-six of the 120 countries in which they are found. And one of the main causes of this alarming rate is the development of shrimp farms. The ecological and community benefits of mangrove habitats seem to be no match for the quick profits that some people seek.

(continued on page 88)

Aerial view of urbanization spreading into the mangrove areas of Kuching, the fourth-largest city in Malaysia. Nicknamed "Cat City," Kuching is situated on the banks of the Sarawak River on the northwestern part of the island of Borneo.

Your Favorite Seafood

How do you like your shrimp? Baked, barbecued, grilled, or stir-fried, shrimp have become a favorite at restaurants and in kitchens across the Western world. The little crustacean is the top-selling seafood in the United States, passing canned tuna in 2001. The shrimp-farming industry is now worth an estimated $60 billion globally. The largest consumer of shrimp, per capita, is Japan.

Most of the farmed shrimp is produced in developing countries in tropical regions such as Southeast Asia. These countries now have some 110,000 warm-water shrimp farms, covering around 3.2 million acres. The five leading countries in the world are Thailand, China, Indonesia, India, and Vietnam.

Shrimp farming is not new to southern Asia. Indonesians have used water ponds called *tambaks* that date back to the fifteenth century. These were mostly small operations found in coastal waters or along river banks. The growth of shrimp farms came later. Development of coastal aquaculture for shrimp farming had its beginning in the late 1960s or early 1970s. Technological advances and global market demand led to a boom in the shrimp industry. Today, about 75 percent of farmed shrimp is produced in Asia—Thailand, Indonesia,

and India are among the world's top producers. The other 25 percent is produced in coastal regions of Central and South America. The majority of these shrimp farms have replaced the natural mangrove forests in those regions.

Aquaculture in many coastal countries is a critical economic activity. It offers employment, community development, food security, and in many locations poverty alleviation. But according to one estimate, 38 percent of recent mangrove loss is attributable to the development of shrimp aquaculture. A report by the London-based Environmental Justice Foundation claims "the West's appetite for jumbo-size tiger shrimp (tiger prawns) is degrading the environmental health of many of the world's poorest nations." The report sights the loss of coastal mangrove forests, loss of wildlife habitat, and increased use of antibiotics and pesticides as some of the problems.

Annabelle Aish, a marine researcher with the Environmental Justice Foundation, advises consumers to "cut down on eating shrimp, or cut it out altogether—unless you can be assured it comes from sustainable sources. Consumers have considerable power and responsibility." ∎

The future of the mangrove ecosystem is changing. Most countries have enacted new rules that restrict the conversion of mangroves for aquaculture and they assess the impact on the environment before using mangroves areas for other development. "This has led to better protection and management of mangroves in some countries," Wulf Killmann, director of FAO'S Forest Products and Industry Division, stated. "But overall, the loss of these coastal forests remains alarming. The rate of mangrove loss is significantly higher that the loss of any other types of forests."

Message of Hope - Communities Restoring Mangroves Forests

On the western tropical coast of Africa, the country of Senegal is attempting to reverse the deforestation of the mangrove forest by planting mangrove trees. Not hundreds, not even thousands, but 6 million mangroves have been planted. The mangroves were declining in the southern regions of Senegal when up to 15,000 youths from 130 villages helped in this massive planting. The goal is not only to restore the mangroves but in the process boost fishing success and revive the livelihoods of the community members. John Eichelsheim, project manager of the local organization Intervene, Development, Ecology and Environment stated, "The more mangroves there are here, the more fish, shrimp and oysters there will be to eat and sell." The restored mangroves will also help to protect the villages from storm damage and increase habitat for wildlife.

The project started in 2008, so its success will not be seen for five to ten years. Nevertheless, the group is moving forward by seeking legislation from the Senegalese government to establish national laws to protect the mangrove forests. And, officials have recommended close study to determine the types of mangroves to plant and how to make the project successful over a long period of time. ■

Chapter Six
Sustainable Forests

I t was during the *mbura ya njahi*—the season of long rains, in 1940, that Wangari Maathai was born in the central highlands of Kenya. As a girl, Maathai loved listening to birds and would help her mother collect firewood. Wood and water were abundant during her childhood. She also enjoyed gardening and working the soil.

However, by the time Maathai had finished all her schooling, including earning a Master of Science from the University of Pittsburgh and a Ph.D. from the University of Nairobi, Kenya, her community had changed. The land around her community was like a desert, because the topsoil had blown away. During the *mbura ya njahi*, soil erosion was great and the streams silted. The farmers in the region had been encouraged to raise cash crops like tea and coffee for export and had cut down the abundant fig trees. The trees, bushes, and grasses in which Maathai had played during her youth were gone. Even her favorite fig tree had been chopped down.

Maathai also observed a change in the people, especially their diets. A researcher had concluded that a shortage of firewood limited the ability to cook and this was leading to malnutrition—most noticeable among children and the elderly. Deforestation of the area had led to many challenges, both socially and environmentally.

Maathai decided to do something. She organized the women of the community, a high percentage of whom were illiterate, and taught them to plant trees. She started a nursery for native species and paid locals four cents for every tree they planted and cared for. Thirty years and 30 million trees later, Maathai won the 2004 Nobel Peace Prize for her efforts to reforest her native Kenya. "It's the little things citizens do," said Maathai, whose Green Belt Movement is a model for reforesting the

Two Kenyan women planting trees as part of the Green Belt Movement

world. "That's what will make the difference. My little thing is planting trees."

A world away, in Washington, D.C., Betty Brown Casey read a *Washington Post* article that moved her to plant trees. The *Post* report said that the District of Columbia had lost 64 percent of its tree cover between the mid-1970s and 1997. Casey donated $50 million to establish an endowment for Casey Trees, a nonprofit dedicated to restoring, enhancing, and protecting the tree canopy in the nation's capital. Casey Trees planted 1,500 trees in 2007 and has set a goal of reaching a 40 percent Urban Tree Canopy in twenty-five years.

The Urban Tree Canopy (UTC) is defined as the layer of leaves, branches, and stems in an urban area that cover

Wangari Maathai

the ground when viewed from above. Across the United States, cities have an average tree canopy cover of 27.1 percent. But mayors of many cities in the United States have established tree planting goals for their communities. The cities of Los Angeles, New York, Denver, and Salt Lake City have established the goal of planting a million trees.

Urban areas occupy 3.5 percent of the total land area in the United States. Yet, 80 percent of Americans live in urban areas (cities, towns, or villages with at least 2,500 people). The value of trees in these areas benefits a community in different ways. Landscaping, especially with trees, can significantly increase property values. A value of 9 percent ($15,000) was determined in a U.S. tax court case for the loss of a large black oak on a property valued at $164,500. Trees also reduce runoff and erosion from storms by about 7 percent and reduce the need for erosion control structures.

A study by the Center for Urban Horticulture at the University of Washington shows that a mature tree canopy in a city reduces air temperatures by 5° to 10° F, lessening the need for air conditioning. A mature tree absorbs 120 to 240 pounds of air pollution's small particles and gases each year. The U.S. Department of Agriculture also reports that one acre of forest absorbs six tons of carbon dioxide and puts out four tons of oxygen.

The forested regions of the earth are under great pressure from a growing population, a need for products, and a climate that is changing. We continue to deforest regions of the earth, and degrade remaining forest areas at an alarming rate. The result is that forests are jeopardized. But sustainable forest management means different things to different people. Not everyone agrees on how best to preserve the world's forested areas, and forest sustainability is a very complex issue. Moreover, there are many key global issues that will impact the results of forest sustainability. The possible effects of climate change, for example, may increase the incidence and severity of forest fires and pest and disease infestation and

i-Tree Streets

What is the value of a tree in the urban environment? A state-of-the-art, peer reviewed software suite developed by the USDA Forest Service provides urban forestry analysis on the benefits and services that trees provide. Individual urban tree values can be calculated by using data collected by citizen scientists or students. The data required is the species name and the size of the tree, which is determined by measuring the diameter at breast height (DBH) of every tree in the area being studied. After entering the data at i-Tree (http://www. itreetools.org) you will be able to determine a dollar value for each tree entered. The field-tested program will consider the following benefits when determining the total value of that specific tree: storm water, property value, energy, air quality, and CO_2. The program also allows you to look to the future. You can enter a larger size of the tree and see what the value will be in the future. ■

may alter forest ecosystems. At the same time, concern about climate change will focus increased attention on the role of forests in carbon conservation and sequestration and in substitution of fossil fuels.

Globally, the importance of forests has reached an international level of awareness. A resolution adopted by the United Nations General Assembly has designated 2011 the International Year of Forests. And, the United Nations Environment Programme (UNEP) has launched a worldwide tree planting campaign.

The "Plant for the Planet: Billion Tree Campaign" challenges individuals and communities to plant at least 1 billion trees worldwide each year. Tree planters are encouraged to investigate the best type of tree to plant for the site selected, and they're encouraged to plant indigenous trees. So far, people have planted more than 4 billion trees. Former Vice President Al Gore has said, "The symbolism—and the substantive significance—of planting a tree has universal power in every culture and every society on Earth, and it is a way for individual men, women and children to participate in creating solutions for the environmental crisis."

(continued on page 100)

Youth Involvement

In the village of Uaxactún in Guatemala, fourteen-year-old Lusvin Pop takes care of 400 plants, which—after weekly care of almost a year—will be transplanted in a rain forest.

Lusvin is one of many boys in his community who perform this work and learn about the management and propagation of *xate* (pronounced SHA-tay). The forest in which Lusvin will transplant the *xate* is a two-hour walk from where he lives, but he doesn't mind and neither does his teacher. "It delights me that the children are actively involved in the environment," Lusvin's teacher, Victor Emilio Quixchan, said. "We depend on the forest; the forest does not depend on us. We must preserve the natural resources the forests have because they provide a fountain of income for all the families here in the community."

Uaxactún (pronounced Wash-ahk-TUN) is a small village of about 140 families. Uaxactún's families are responsible for 206,390 acres of land—98 percent of it forested. The villagers do not own the forest land, but have permission

Lusvin Pop

from the government to harvest products from it. They collect allspice and *xate* palm leaves (used by florists in the United States); cut vines and weave them into wicker furniture; and selectively log mahogany trees, selling the lumber and keeping the twigs and leaves to fertilize the forest floor.

Each harvest demands careful balance. Cut the *xate* frond in the wrong place, the plant dies. Bend the pepper plant too far, the stem breaks. Slide a machete blade too deeply into the chicozapote bark, insects invade and destroy. Fell too many large trees, in floods too much heat and light. Much of the forest floor's life withers without the essential, dim dampness provided by the canopy.

The Rainforest Alliance has helped the community to find sustainable products and markets for these products. And, the community is doing so well that is has been able to open a high school and start a new plant nursery. Said Lusvin: "I am very proud to help the community and I feel I am learning respect for nature and our natural resources." ■

Ana Maria Caal prepares the xate for shipping.

According to the World Bank, "more than 1.6 billion people depend to varying degrees on forests for their livelihoods. Forest resources directly contribute to the livelihoods of 90 percent of the 1.2 billion people living in extreme poverty and indirectly support the natural environment that nourishes agriculture and food supplies of nearly half the population in the developed world. Some 1 billion people worldwide depend on drugs derived from forest plants for their medicinal needs. Worldwide, forest industries provide employment for 60 million people."

Global forestry trends suggest that deforestation and forest degradation will continue in most developing regions, because wood will remain the most important source of energy. In Africa, for example, wood provides almost 90 percent of its energy use. A reversal of the situation would depend on shifts in economies to reduce direct and indirect dependence on land. In contrast, deforestation has stopped in parts of Asia and the Pacific, Europe, and North America—regions where the agricultural land base has shrunk; though, the rising price of oil and increasing concern for climate change may result in increased use of wood as fuel in both developed and developing countries.

Meanwhile, planted forests continue to increase dramatically on every continent other than Africa. The wood production from planted forests is approaching 50 percent of total wood production. In 2005, two countries, China and India, had more than 55 percent of the world's planted forests. China, in particular, is committed to planting forests because the country is the world's biggest consumer of wood.

Since domestic logging was restricted in China in 1998, the volume of wood entering China has risen nine-fold. This demand has accelerated illegal deforestation in Russia, South America, Africa, and Indonesia. The biggest supplier by far is Russia, which provides 60 percent of the logs that come into China. As buildings go up in Beijing, Shanghai, Guangzhou, and Chongqing, the vast boreal forests of Siberia are being reduced.

Certification of Forest Products

How can a consumer identify if the wood product he or she is purchasing comes from a managed sustainable forest? Production companies and retailers have started to identify products through a process called "certification." Certification ensures that a wood product or other forest resource has met a certain set of environmental and social guidelines. This certification takes into account a number of factors, such as compliance with all relevant laws and international treaties; the rights and interests of the workers, communities, and indigenous peoples involved in the harvesting of the wood; chemical use; and whether the wood is from a rare, threatened, or endangered species.

Forestry operations that meet the standards are granted certification and audited annually. Forestry operations are required to make improvements as a condition of getting certified and staying certified over time. This annual assessment ensures that products sold as certified actually originate in certified forests.

Forest certification has been established as a forest management tool for more than a decade and nearly 740 million acres have been certified under credible, audited programs. Despite this progress, much of the world's forests, especially in tropical regions, continue to face over-exploitation, conversion to agriculture, and massive human-caused wildfires. What's more, only about 9 percent of the world's forest area is certified, and most of these forests are in temperate or boreal regions where forest area is relatively stable and not subjected to the threats facing tropical forests. ■

At current harvesting rates, the Russian far east could be logged out in 20 years, according to a study by the Beijing Forestry University.

In 1949, American ecologist, forester, and environmentalist Aldo Leopold wrote a book of essays in which he outlined a new "land ethic" to guide people in their relationship with nature. "We abuse land because we regard it as a commodity belonging to us," Leopold explained. "When we see land as a community to which we belong, we may begin to use it with love and respect."

Leopold earned a masters degree in forestry from Yale in 1909 and then worked for the U.S. Forest Service for nineteen years. He was an early visionary and advocate of forest stewardship. Though he died in 1948, at the age of sixty-one, his ideas are still relevant today. His book, *A Sand County Almanac*, sells about 40,000 copies a year and has been translated into nine languages.

In one passage of the book, Leopold addressed the question of what is a conservationist. Within the answer to this question, he also answered another one, which scientists, environmentalists, and ordinary people grapple with today: how does this generation protect, preserve, and manage forests for future generations? Wrote Leopold,

I have read many definitions of what is a conservationist, and written not a few myself, but I suspect that the best one is written not with a pen, but with an axe. It is a matter of what a man thinks about while chopping, or while deciding what to chop. A conservationist is one who is humbly aware that with each stroke he is writing his signature on the land.

Sources

Chapter One: The Forest Planet

p. 21, "Today, because of pressure . . ." Nature Conservancy, "The Boreal Forests: Scientists Call for the Preservation of the Boreal," http://www.nature.org/wherewework/northamerica/Canada/work/art12507.html.

Chapter Two: Deforestation: The Human Impacts

p. 27, "It seems that . . ." David A. Perry, Ram Oren, and Stephen C. Hart, *Forest Ecosystems,* 2nd ed. (Baltimore: Johns Hopkins University Press, 2008), 5.

p. 29, "the settlers of Easter . . ." Julie Wasson, "Harming Environment Leads to Society Collapse," *Blue Planet Green Living*, February 5, 2009. http://www.organicgreeandnatural.com/2009/02/05/harming-environment-leads-to-societal-collapse.

p. 29, "The spread of agriculture . . ." Peter Thomas and John R. Packham, *Ecology of Woodlands and Forests: Description, Dynamics, and Diversity* (Cambridge: Cambridge University Press, 2007), 4.

p. 29, "People have been deforesting . . ." Perry, *Forest Ecosystems,* 5.

p. 32, "the production and consumption . . ." Food and Agriculture Organization of the United Nations, *State of the World's Forests 2009* (Food and Agriculture Organization of the United Nations, 2009), 69.

p. 34, "overconsumption by consumers . . ." World Rainbow Movement, "What are Underlying Causes of Deforestation?" in *The World Guide 1999/2000*, Oxford, U.K.: New Internationalists Publications, Ltd.

p. 34, "Forests are thus being . . ." World Rainbow Movement, "What are Underlying Causes of Deforestation?"

p. 37, "Since the early 1970s . . ." Perry, *Forest Ecosystems,* 7.

p. 38, "Despite improved . . ." Rhett Butler, "Logging." http://rainforests/Mongabay.com/0807.htm.

p. 39, "When the annual use . . ." Alain Marcoux, "Population and Deforestation," Sustainable Development Department, Food and Agriculture Organization of the United Nations, August 2000, http://www.fao.org/sd/wpdirect/Wpan0050.htm.

p. 46, "A significant part . . ." Renee Maltezou and Dina Kyriakidou, "Wildfire Rages Near Athens, Thousands Flee," Reuters, August 23, 2009, http://www.reuters.com/article/latestCrisis/idUSLN 250275.

p. 48, "A lot of insects . . ." Scott Kirkwood, "A Burning Question," *National Parks Magazine*, Summer 2005, http://www.npca.org/magazine/2005/summer/mysteries.html.

p. 48, "People usually do not . . ." Western Fire Ecology Center/American Lands Alliance, "Introduction to Fire Ecology," http://www.fire- ecology.org/education/doc1.htm.

Chapter Three: U.S. Forests: Changes Over Time

p. 49, "laden with good . . ." Porter E. Sargent, *A Handbook of New England*, 2nd ed. (Boston: Porter E. Sargent, 1917), 49.

p. 50, "Oakes . . ." Michael Williams, *Americans & Their Forests: A Historical Geography* (Cambridge: Cambridge University Press, 1989), 22.

p. 50, "[He] fells the forests . . ." Ibid., 5.

p. 51, "Their houses are . . ." Ibid., 40.

p. 53, "in 1850, there were . . ." Douglas W. MacCleery, *American Forests: A History of Resiliency and Recovery* (Durham, NC: Forest History Society, 1991), 16.

p. 53, "Except for the engine . . ." Ibid.

p. 54, "cheap bread . . ." Williams, *Americans & Their Forests: A Historical Geography,* 490.

p. 55, "There are few . . ." Ibid., 371.

p. 56, "the greatest good . . ." Williams, *Americans & Their Forests: A Historical Geography,* 420.

p. 58, "Almost 60 percent . . ." *Working Solutions for Conservation,* 2007 Annual Report of the American Forestry Foundation.

p. 61, "never before did . . ." John Muir, *The Mountains of California* (University of California Press, 1989), 191.

Chapter Four: Amazonia: Deforestation of a Global Forest

p. 72, "The first accidental . . ." Rebecca Lindsey, "From Forest to Field: How Fire is Transforming the Amazon," *Earth Observatory*, June 8, 2004.

p. 74, "the soybean farmers . . ." Eric Jackson, "What are the Most Important Factors that Drive Amazonia's deforestation?," Panama News, February 7, 2004.

p. 74, "We are determined . . ." Raymond Colitt, "Brazil Targets Illegal Logging in Raid in Amazon," Reuters, April 8, 2009.

p. 75, "While Amazonia . . ." United Nations Environment Programme and Amazon Cooperation Treaty Organization, *Environmental Outlook in the Amazonia: GEO Amazonia*, 2008.

p. 76, "The indigenous . . ." Ibid.

p. 76, "It's our strong belief . . ." Rhett A. Butler, interview with ethnobotanist Dr. Mark Plotkin, Mongabay.com, October 31, 2006, http://news.mongabay.com/2006/1031-interview_plotkin.html.

p. 78, "indigenous territories have proved. . ." Barbara Zimmerman, "Commentary: A Burning Issue," Conservation International, May 19, 2008, http://www.conservation.org/FMG/Articles/Pages/zimmerman_indigenous_climate_change.aspx.

p. 78, "Indigenous territories . . ." Ibid.

Chapter Five: The Disappearing Mangroves: The Tidal Forest

p. 80, "The tsunami . . ." "Mangroves Shielded Communities Against Tsunami," *Science Daily*, October 28, 2005.

p. 84, "Encroachment into mangrove . . ." "Loss of Mangrove Forests Increased Cyclone Damage," *Science News*, redOrbit.com, May 8, 2008, www.redorbit.com/ news/ science/ 1375821/ loss_of_mangrove_forests_increased_cyclone_damage/.

p. 87, "the West's appetite . . ." James Owen, "Shrimp's Success Hurts Asian Environment, Group Says," National Geographic News, December 20, 2004, http:// news.nationalgeographic.com/news/2004/06/0621_040621_shrimpfarm.html.

p. 87, "cut down on eating shrimp . . ." Ibid.

p. 88, "This has led . . ." "UN: Mangrove Forest Vanishing at an 'Alarming' Rate," Environment News Service, February 3, 2008, http//www.protectingourenvironment.com/ un-mangrove-forests-vanishing-at-an-alarming-rate/.

p. 89, "The more mangroves . . ." "Senegal: Protecting livelihoods through mangroves," October 14, 2008, AlertNet.org, Thomson Reuters Foundation, http://www.alertnet.org/ thenews/ newsdesk/ IRIN/ d2e5bbe9dfa22c9a29675400ea01f7a9.htm.

Chapter Six: Sustainable Forests

p. 92, "It's the little things . . ." Stephanie Hayes, "Nobel Prize Winner: Small Steps Change the World," *St. Petersburg Times*, March 24, 2006.

p. 96, "The symbolism . . ." Albert Gore, *Earth in the Balance: Ecology and the Human Spirit*, rev. ed. (New York, NY: Houghton Mifflin Harcourt, 2000), 323.

p. 98, "It delights me . . ." Victor Emilio Quixchan, in discussion with author, March 26, 2009.

p. 99, "I am very proud . . ." Lusvin Pop, in discussion with author, March 26, 2009.

p. 100, "more than 1.6 billion . . ." World Bank, *Sustaining Forests: A Development Strategy* (Washington, D.C.: World Bank 2004), 16.

p. 100, "Forest resources directly . . ." Ibid., 1.

p. 100, "Some 1 billion . . ." Ibid, 16.

p. 100, "Worldwide, forest industries . . ." Ibid.

p. 102, "We abuse land . . ." Aldo Leopold, *A Sand County Almanac and Sketches Here and There*, ed. Robert Finch (New York: Oxford University Press, 1989), viii.

p. 102, "I have read many . . ." Ibid., 168.

Bibliography

Bragaw, Don. "What is Deforestation?" *Issues in Global Education.* http://www.globaled.org/issues/152/a.html.

Butler, Rhett. "Beef drives 80% of Amazon deforestation." Mongabay.com, January 29, 2009, http://news.mongabay.com/2009/0129-brazil.htm.

———. "Logging." Mongabay.com, June 3, 2009, http://rainforests.mongabay.com/0807.htm

Collins, Jocelyn. "Deforestation." *UWC EnviroFacts.* February 2001, http://www.botany.uwc.ac.za/envFacts/facts/deforestation.htm.

Cox, Thomas R. *This Well-wooded Land: Americans and Their Forests from Colonial Times to the Present.* Lincoln: University of Nebraska Press, 1985.

Environmental Justice Foundation. "Mangroves: Nature's Defence Against Tsumamis." Environmental Justice Foundation, London, UK, 2006.

Food and Agriculture Organization of the United Nations. *State of the World's Forests*, 2009, http://www.fao.org/docrep/011/i0350e/i0350e00.htm.

Global Warming Science. "Deforestation: The Leading Cause of CO2 Emissions." June 4, 2009, http://www.appinsys.com/GlobalWarming/Deforestation.htm.

Green Facts. "Scientific Facts on Desertification." 2006, http://www.greenfacts.org/en/desertification/index.htm.

———. "Scientific Facts on Forests and Energy." 2009, http://www.greenfacts.org/en/forests-energy/.

———. "What Role Can Forestry and Agriculture Play in Energy Production?" http://www.greenfacts.org/en/forests-energy/index.htm#1.

Innes Productions. "Effects of Deforestation." December 3, 1996, http://trailfire.com/pages/form.php aid=check&bubble=270257.

Kirkwood, Scott K. "A Burning Question." *National Parks Magazine*, Summer 2005.

Leopold, Aldo. *A Sand County Almanac and Sketches Here and There, ed. Robert Finch.* New York, NY: Oxford University Press, 1989.

Marcoux, Alain. "Population and Deforestation." Sustainable Development Department. Food and Agriculture Organization of the United Nations. August 2000, http://www.fao.org/sd/wpdirect/Wpan0050.htm.

MacCleery, Douglas W. *American Forests: A History of Resiliency and Recovery.* Durham, NC: Forest History Society, 1991.

Mongabay.com. "Attacking the Demand Side of Deforestaton." June 16, 2009, http://news.mongabay.com/2009/0615-forest_disclosure.htm.

Muir, John. *The Mountains of California*. University of California Press, 1989.

National Geographic. "Deforestation and Desertification: Forest Holocaust." http://www.nationalgeographic.com/eye/deforestation/effect.html.

Owen, James. "Shrimp's Success Hurts Asian Environment, Group Says," National Geographic News, December 20, 2004, http:// news.nationalgeographic.com/news/2004/06/0621_040621_shrimpfarm.html.

Perlin, John. *A Forest Journal: The Role of Wood in the Development of Civilization*. New York: W. W. Norton, 1989.

Perry, David A., Ram Oren, and Stephen C. Hart. *Forest Ecosystems*. 2nd ed. Baltimore: Johns Hopkins University Press, 2008.

RAND. "Population and Environment: A Complex Relationship." Population Matters Policy Brief. 2000, http://www.rand.org/pubs/research_briefs/RB5045/Index1.html.

Reuters. "Athens Fire Rages Out of Control." August 23, 2009.

Sill, Sute. "Reforesting Michoacan." *American Forests,* Winter 2009.

Thomas, Peter, and John R. Packham. *Ecology of Woodlands and Forests: Description, Dynamics, and Diversity*. Cambridge University Press, 2007.

Wassen, Julie. "Harming Environment Leads to Environmental Collapse," *Blue Planet Green Living*. February 5, 2009. http://www.organicgreenandnatural.com/tag/easter-island/.

World Bank, *Sustaining Forests: A Development Strategy*. Washington, D.C.: World Bank, 2004.

World Rainforest Movement. "What are Underlying Causes of Deforestation?" in *The World Guide 1999/2000*. Oxford, U.K: New Internationalists Publications, Ltd., http://www.wrm.org.uy/deforestation/indirect.html.

World Wildlife Fund. "Forests: Why It Matters." http://www.worldwildlife.org/what/globalmarkets/forests/whyitmatters.html.

Williams, Michael. *Americans and Their Forests: A Historical Geography*. Cambridge University Press, 1989.

Youngquist, W. G., and H. O. Fleischer. *Wood in American Life*. Madison, Wis.: Forest Products Research Society, 1977.

Web sites

American Forests: A Tree for Every Child
http://www.americanforests.org/resources/kids/a_tree_for_every_child/

Food and Agriculture Organization of the United Nations
http://www.fao.org/foresty/home/en

U.S. Forest Service
http://www.fs.fed.us

A Student Guide to Tropical Forest Conservation
http://www.fs.fed.us/global/lzone/student/tropical.htm

Conservation Internationalists
http://www.conservation.org/learn/forests/Pages/overview.aspx

Bill Moyers Reports: Earth on Edge
http://www.pbs.org/earthonedge/ecosystems/forests1.html

American Forest Foundation and Project Learning Tree
http://www.plt.org

Rainforest Alliance
http://www.rainforest-alliance.org

Tree Benefits.com
http://www.treebenefits.com/calculator/

World Forestry Center
http://www.worldforestry.org

Photo Credits

Index

E

F

G

H

I

J

K